Oedipal Dreams

Oedipal Dreams
EVELYN LAU

COACH HOUSE PRESS
TORONTO

Coach House Press
50 Prince Arthur Ave., Suite 107
Toronto, Canada M5R 1B5

© 1992, 1994 Evelyn Lau.

SECOND EDITION

First edition published by Beach Holme Publishers 1992
Second edition published by Coach House Press 1994
First American Edition published by Coach House Press 1994

Printed in Canada

Canadian Cataloguing in Publication Data

Lau, Evelyn, 1971–
    Oedipal dreams

Poems.
ISBN 0-88910-490-5

I. Title.

PS8573.A781504 1994   C811'.54   C94-930857-9
PR9199.3.L3804 1994

Acknowledgments

Some of the poems in this collection first appeared in the following magazines and anthologies:

Ariel, Best American Poetry 1992, Hawaii Review, Humane Medicine, League of Canadian Poets Anthology, Living the Changes, Michigan Quarterly Review, The New Quarterly, Prairie Fire, Prism International, Queen's Quarterly, Tampa Review and *Vancouver Review.*

Contents

In Search of You in Search of Freud

we talk of emotional corrective experiences
of secondary elaborations during afternoon drives
I listen to your Czechoslovakian analyst's accent
her impressive business card titles, I unfold your money
from cards with endearments inside
maddened by my reluctance to become a composite
of mother and girlfriends and wives
before they tipped over their pedestals
you stop by the side of the road where cups of rain
spill over into sand and mud
you are like one of Freud's
unscrupulous nurses who calm crying children to sleep
by stroking their genitals

nights I squirm over textbooks
punch pillows and slam down dictionaries
recognize you anywhere neurosis is discussed
still I fantasize penetrating the sunken echelons of your profession
still I imagine walking beside you through filters of air
into medical conventions where your aged heroes lecture
with eyes so hungry they have eaten their patients
you forgive them as though they are your parents
write articles to defend them
only in your dreams do they become a monster tearing
and clawing at the bathroom door you hid behind as a child
from your father, only in your dreams
do you tell the truth

we travel across borders with careless guards willing to trust
in the pattern of your tie,

when I touch you, you feel as I imagine a ghost must,
clothed, hollow, a chill rush of air
I torture your already subdued body with words
lines thick and rubbery as whips
I long to snap the skeleton of you
to rub your dispassionately analytical eyes into black and bone
uncrowded by thought
smoothed sleepy as genitalia

The Lost Hours

in dreams where you walk I am a pale scar around your neck
a leaf twisting about your ankles, I am between the fingers
you rub together, betraying a desire to take notes
25 years of taking notes in analysis and the gesture comes to you
like a blink or a tense muscle.
I have kept the lost hours
the nights you thought I gave to needles
and the snowflake scatter of white pills
—they cause amnesia, you said, and the truth to come out—
your hands reached out gloved in softness to gather up
the babble of truth that slipped from my mouth in a rush
of polished stones, marbles.

you thought I'd lost hours like trinkets while you were busy
driving home through a blizzard of night
and a cold that stuck itself to you like a wet tongue
thrust against an iron gate in winter
you abandoned loneliness for an office-party where you insisted
the nurses lined up to press their bodies against yours
I wonder what you wore?
your patients escaped through a black corridor with seeking hands
balleting around their faces
their hands fluttered art above the chair I fell into.
you pocketed the hours, I spent them freely
and walked with you into imaginary havens, saw you serious
with a sunken lip, saw that same lip grasping another
tasting of lipstick and tears and confessions.

I have held the lost hours in my own dry palm
I have sought them and it has been like looking for

something buried on a beach after dark, I have been looking,
combing back the hairs of the afternoon.
all your lost people thrum in the darkness of my night
I have had to learn to forgive each one
often they had delicate hair
the first whiff of defeat had been ironed into their clothes
already their eyes had gone.
why did you leave it so long?
the two Chinese lamps in your office held nothing back
the floor was awash with the layers of your suit, we were
struggling to learn something or to forget everything
beneath books by Freud and Havelock Ellis and some new
Californian psychologist.
you had written me into your appointment book with initials
that were not my own.
I counted the hours into my purse and wrote the important names
into a black book in the bathroom
and laughed all the way back down the long hallway to your office
because you were smiling where you stood.

Half

he came down to you from the ceiling
a ruinous god descending from his machine, flat-footed
wearing a bedsheet and a rotted smile
but a god nonetheless
this was the beginning of half a year, a long time
in a life so short as yours
so easily bought with clothing money or taxi fare or next month's rent
you sold out for promises, simple things like checks in the mail
and sacrificial things like a divorce
a house the two of you would choose together
he said he'd been contemplating what to take with him
what to tell his lawyer
what to tell his wife
asleep in the bathtub, head bent heavy on the rim
black hair snaking in a tweedy rope down her shoulder
her voice on the phone cultivated
a proper doctor's wife voice
you hung up
though he was not far away, count seven miles
and the minutes that wound down to six months being a long time
you gave him what he wanted
you gave him some time
and your conviction that a modern day deus ex machinas
never looked so good, never smelled so clean
you believed that all your men and your heatless sexual acts
were meant to be rewarded with the moment
a god fell from the sky in a cardboard box
you thought you'd chased down the dream
because he climbed out and told you Yes
and I love you, and a house to call your own

or at least half a house
half of something

Touring the Ward

in the cafeteria you stood staring at yourself
the striated tie and that raspberry stain from lunch
like a bloom on your shirt, like a torn heart
in the mirrored windows that kept out the lawns and the ocean
the tongue-lapping of waves.
looking at the windows you saw your own aged face
and somewhere, far back, maybe mine: pale with drug,
with the tiny brown bottles and the happy squirt of the needle.
you shouldered into your jacket and showed me your ward
rooms with limp curtains and pillows
offices with poor fringes on the lamps, and chairs
where men sat writing prescriptions all day.
a woman tagged eight feet behind us in a jean jacket
smelling of cigarettes, she had sharp eyes and cheeks
scored with lines.
her runners slapped up and down on the floor.
I toured the ward with you, step for step, you smiled furiously
and extended hands when all the patients
shuffled out of their chairs and beds and their malaise
to crowd around you and call you Doctor.
their eyes slanted jealously at me,
my footsteps had matched yours from the exercise room
to the isolation rooms to the exit doors
where with one hand you pulled me straight into the twilight outside
the green outer skin of the world.
the woman in the jean jacket pressed against the doors,
shadows around her eyes and a knife
tucked in each corner of her mouth.
I remembered five years ago, two doctors walking side by side
through a different ward, laughing, they had the round faces

of boys as they walked past a woman in a wig
who drank a cup of ice cream with panicked eyes.
their feet were perfectly in step.
when we left I followed you to your car, your shoes were newly polished
they shone like the skins of apples, you were swinging
the keys to your car and house and hospital
quoting Goethe, quoting Freud
pointing at the few weak stars and walking ahead.

Waiting for a Ride Out of Here

at this corner of 7-ll's, parking lots
grocery stores with apartments upstairs
the dust of the evening sits in her nostrils
the wind slides down the back of her shirt
she watches women walking their dogs and each other
cars that roll towards her with firefly eyes
she waits for a car with one broken headlight
this was the instruction, this is all
she knows
pairs of headlights sweep yellow silk down the sidewalk
missing her feet like a wave
she sees now why he has chosen this part of town
the only corner of beauty
is near the airport, where the planes fly out
and bugs fly up in a golden storm from roads and bushes
here he watches the planes escape
into some blue place of vanishing
when they are high and lost he turns the car around
follows the lines in his mind, all pointing away from her

Coming and Going

and so you return
it is noon and your face at the door
seems familiar enough — cheekbones and nose and a mouth
reaching up for a smile
our tongues question each other
funny new lines hatch your eyelids

I draw the drapes
against this blue smoggy afternoon
worry each of your words, mentally flip
1000-page Freudian textbooks to analyze their origins
unfasten two slender silver hooks
and a trouser button
my hands settle on islands of flesh rising
above the sailing layers of your suit

impossible to hold on to
the tangled sheets and slow-motion bodies
the curlicue of incense
unfinished mugs of tea on the kitchen table
your eyes never rest, I watch our complexities
twine like sunburnt arms in their shallows

you look younger here but then
there is that moment at the door
when the sun clanks its cage down around us again
our hands imprisoned in each other's
when the light scrapes your face pale as a belly
and the mid-afternoon guides you away
with sensual polluted fingers

The Second Waiting Room

you sit waiting with arms locked against a box of light
edging out the shape of your body in the chair, eyes
staring into winter sunlight
you have feet like a woman's, ankles tangled beneath the desk
and a crack in the leather shoes, the eye of the revealed sock
demure and egg-blue

you reached into your pocket once and dropped a coin
into the golden dragon's belly
in the caverns of its rusted green body it had sounded
like a handful jangling down
and from that day on all my money began to smell of you
even that hundred dollar bill.
I struggled to breathe you into me.
it was only afterwards in the unwrapping, the stubborn furled edges
the bend down the centre of the bill
that I smelled not some chemical but you
you bled out of my nose for days

in the bar with the waitress whose lips played grim at the sight of you
you refused to take off your trenchcoat
amongst the men in baseball caps and Harley Davidson shirts
the tie and tweed suit would not have gone over well
later you pointed beneath your black nipple
 the scar shaped like a smile
I turned protectively in my seat, the men's eyes at my back
took your impulsive shaking fingers, the released buttons falling away
too quickly to pin them back

in your office you sit beneath the painting with the dark-haired man
bent down to the woman, the one with the hair

she seems to be caught in
her hands press out as if at the sides of a glass box
white flowers of bewilderment
his olive eyelids stoop to cover his expression
his hands are too busy gentling her body to notice
she seems to be drowning
his mouth catches hers like teeth catching a lower lip
puncturing a hot salt of blood
and meanwhile the breast-white stars and moon circle above them
and above you, heedlessly, round and round

Dream

fog slipped over the ocean like a skirt
over a woman's thighs, we were on a ferry with pairs of lovers
standing on the deck below us, and policemen
leaning on steel ladders, eating sandwiches. and though
this was to be the end, your hands were empty,
your patients sat in booths around us with crossed legs,
and when I pried your hands open you rose,
stooping into the faces of your patients,
your hand on the backs of their chairs to reassure them
or to support yourself.

they caught your tie in their hands, they looked at you
with eyes the shapes of plastic flowers, their mouths
stretched with hope. your hands were empty,
I pushed away from the table
and escaped to your medicine chest
stealing boxes and bottles of drugs, you came and watched,
hands in pockets in the doorway. I saw you and ran
to the bathroom, ingesting drugs down the hallway,
there was already someone there, I threw up
into his black briefcase, came out with my hands empty
and my smile guiltless.

the fog shouldered in like a beast,
the lovers jumped in pairs into the night,
the policemen laughed and poked each other in the ribs.
your patients huddled in their booths, they were so cold,
you went to them offering handfuls of smiles
while lovers leapt brightly into the night. then this was gone
and you were inside my old high school,

you locked yourself into a classroom while I stood outside
in the centre of the summer day,
the smell of daisies pushing through the air,
the sidewalks paved with hopscotch squares.
the sun ate up the sky and when I looked back
you were behind one of hundreds of windows, I did not know which one,
I was a child in shorts with sand in my mouth,
the sun was ashen and on every street I turned down
the houses were empty.

Only an Abreaction

the office and the furniture won't stop moving, why won't they stop
his hand sails out and you like its brown kiss on your cheek
he turns in the window's stingy light
and asks for it back but your face is a bowl of warm berries
your eyes become simple
he steps out from the far wall with the needle pointing first
at the ceiling, then at your feet
delight in the eyes and the shape of the lips, delight
in the cool drug seeping into you
wet as love
and then laughter, the crystal syringe bright as any day gone by
two lines of moisture in his lower eyelids
you cried, you do not remember crying
—you said you were afraid
—afraid of what?
—whatever it is that most people are afraid of, life maybe
life. it had to be that

the cylinder of the syringe firm between your fingers
you enter him, its toothed point bites his arm
he holds still and points at a freckle and says
There and That one and Push
all you have to do is push
his flesh feels like a silk glove, feels like butter
Freud would have smiled
he lies on the floor a tempered child, arms and legs pointing
in the possible directions, tie bent in a crayon scribble

and now the curving craftiness of his smile.
his eyes floating away on the twin baths of salt liquid.

the dot of lint tangled in the brush of eyelashes.
how large he seems, coming out from behind the bookcase
carrying the needle like an old vase or a precious tray
how puzzlingly smiling
you take the buffed face of Freud between your fingers
try to warm the dead cheeks with your palms
on the shelf a toy clown marches in circles with a key spinning
wildly in its back and a high tone rising, a song
there is a song here after all
he is twisting out the music with his hands.

Eight Months Later: His House

there is a moment of flight in your throat when the key
turns in the lock, and fits
and you follow him inside
a strangled christ dangles on the wall
toy soldiers rally between the bannisters
he keeps a sword beside his empty bed
who is the enemy? how can
the enemy enter and not be frozen
by the blue and white snowflake of this home
a kitchen out of some magazine where kitchens stay
sunny and pine, where the wood is blond
and clusters of dried things smell — herbs, spices, flowers
your pupils spin as if you have stepped
from a black shelter into light
you do not see the three wedding photos on the dresser
where his arm holds a woman who looks happy
even though she is standing in a park by the edge of a cliff
with a good view

Payments

that night in the bar
with the obligatory man in the corner who stared
out of predatory eyes, eyebrows so angry
I knew instinctively sex would be violent
and colorful
I drank to life without you
the scotch took a long time to slide down
the laughter came from other tables

two days later I snuck back
to bi-weekly cash installments
and expensive tax-deductible gifts
to hold you in my arms and watch you cry
into your suit
one hand on the back of my knee
the other over your face
I held you and read the spines of books
on the shelf across the apartment
not feeling much
not used to hearing the sounds people make
when they're made to cry

these psychological S&M games
call for no turned cheeks or dark glasses
no bruises like the ones on the necks of other hookers
no thumbprints the color of coffee spilled
over collars and between the waves of hair
nothing so visible as that
or impermanent
the marks we leave fray at the edges
ache on the inside

my highest bidder yet
you have paranoid eyes and a telltale voice
scaling the keyboard of neuroses
your hands could seldom afford to be empty
even when they didn't know what they were paying for
you wear masks painted black and then
nothing but the cellophane transparency of skin
I fly towards you to relieve your weighted hands
fill them up with kisses and thanks and the necessary
girlish delight
practise the busy eyelashes and wet mouth
of innocence

funny that you should teach me
with your glad tight arms and the cripple that lives
in your eyes
without crutches or canes
that somewhere behind the wall of money
that wrestles us apart
a little light can trickle through
and I might come to know what people talk about
when they talk about love

Bruises

his hands were rough as unpainted walls, his hands
confirmed the presence of a neck between them
the sensation of smooth lily, a curve of hair
each callous a blunt instrument scraping.
his smile was the smallest I had seen. under the staircase
the child in him crouched, the grown man he presented
held a saw with triangular teeth
that simulated the noise of pain.
I tied him on top of the sky-blue comforter
on the bed which staged his adolescent torment.
there was no light, no heat
there were two lines of wet clothes strung from wall to wall
the pockets of the trousers turned out.

hands pressed flat hard marks down my neck
they left the rawness of rope burns, bruises like blackberries.
a red light bulb was screwed in every socket
we swam in a sea of bloody sheets
I touched him as if through cellophane.
my tears pinched his eyes small
caused him to lurch out of bed and crash into the kitchen wall
swearing all the way
his handsome face flattened by rage.
later I swore in a cab all the way home
the offended arm hanging out the window
and the city air tasting of glass.

neither of them reminded me of you until you returned
wearing a fashionable tie, your eyes seemed lost
and when we passed the bottle of pills back and forth

I wanted you to take them all
with me, but each time I shut my lips
when my hand strayed towards my mouth. you must have done the same
because you stayed wide awake, I fell asleep
and dreamt of long scissors in your hands
dreamt that you cut my dress til it fell off in strips of black lace
that you went to the closet for my other clothes, scissors leaping,
and I knew I would be naked soon.

The Other Woman

every womanly sense in me knows
the seduction of the couch
leather against your wool suit
to be headier than my limbs and the way they curl
around your familiar poses
who after all can compete with a good analyst
aged to brilliance
the lamp she tilts on your face offers a gentler caress
than my fingertips
her pen roves silently across paper, my words
are lumpy and pockmarked as dice

she offers you a glass of whiskey
I heard about the girl, she says
why didn't you come to me?
aren't I your friend?
can't you tell me
anything?
and you do
everything
you tell her.
more satisfying than the fleeting entertainment of a visit
to my apartment on your lunch hour
pocket watch fished out and clicked open
eyes preoccupied with an assortment of lies
to explain why lunch can take so long
can smell faintly of cigarettes and perfume
you start at the beginning and tell her and
the same lashes that fluttered scared
like furry feelers against my lips
relax and lie limp as flags

she won't betray you
she is mentor and friend and the mother
who died too soon
I imagine she wears black, that her voice is a wise croak
that the darkness she inhabits
is warm as a womb
needs no paint or perfume or husky bedroom undertones
my power begins to shrivel with the Kleenexes
you twist to ribbons in her office
your home

perhaps she'll tell you
about core conflicts and unipolar depression and something as simple
as mid-life crisis
the leather squeaks its understanding
the couch molds automatically to your form
brown, slick, faintly sweaty, it is still
more trustworthy than flesh
by the end of the session, you'll see
you no longer need your fallen women, your angels
robbed of their halos,
trying to fly
on the strength of one scrawny fibrillating wing

Meeting His Analyst

you were a girl once in a war
holding up a train of laughing soldiers with a tommy gun
chin set like a small white rock
eyes already seeing too far ahead.
your legs were pushed apart, and trembling.
was there a wind, and did your skirt blow
against your knees, and were your hands steady?
you were sixteen, the sky was brown
and the soldiers' laughter clouded your eyes with tears until
the faces blurred, white ghosts under a dirt sky.
the corners of your skirt lashed your legs
the metal burned your fingers
the sun burned a hole in the Czech sky.

when we arrived at the blank face of your home
his fingers closed on your arm, he guided you to the car,
impatience twisted your shoulders, it seemed
he was trying to hold you back with his overcareful hands,
his overeager eyes. the sun was frosty as a mink
in the sky, there was pink in your cheeks, in your lips.

you crowded the lunch table with the names of foreign analysts
he held your words like overripe fruits
played them back to me again and again,
suddenly young and at the same time, my father,
angling for praise. across the table
his mouth widened with love for you, went slack,
the flowers on his tie twitched and bled.
you would not look at me til he left,
your eyes were pointed as gun barrels, and canny.

you might have been sixteen, arms shaking,
eyes permanently twisted sideways with rage
and fright. in the fixed needles of your gaze I was unmysterious,
my hands were skilled and torturing.

when you walked back to the chill face of your house
the sun stood in your eyes
you grew small and smaller behind the thicket of the dead vines
the dead brown garden.
the piano in the living room was silent,
the husband was greeting a patient in the consulting room,
and briefly your hair shone white,
and your skirt blew stripes against your legs.

Your Ending or Mine

in a certain light, with you
bent over so, the sky from behind snarling your hair,
the lines on your face slide into position
the in/out dimpling of that nervous muscle
locked between chin and earlobe
depresses beneath my fingertip, sleepy and hollow
the smell of Polo rims the blankets like salt
crusting a margarita
I dream you grow three unhappy faces
and extract wedding rings that swim up
to the leakage of dawn
your eggshell eyelids open, the sun
squints your pupils shrewd and small

once you came up my stairs like a good thing
with a teeth-showing smile
your suit and tie and the slenderness of your legs
contrived to spell safety
the hand that took mine on the threshold
had reassuring knuckles
that was the beginning, you told about wife and teenage children
two hours later your mouth was on my pillow

now you arrive with money and books and on a good day,
drugs
to put me to sleep through supper
launch me clear through til grey evening, the drapes open
upon a parking lot and an alley
the only lights way off beyond touching
after waking I begin the experimental first step

stagger in scarves of dizziness
disrobe the fairy tale into non-fiction

the cruelty of the affair is kaleidoscopic
a turning wheel of colored sand and broken glass
triangular windows of possibility
hours spent nursing the stomach-dropping illness of love
not knowing what to do with this new thing
except swallow it down where you can't extract it
hold it up twisting in your hands like some
ghostly/ghastly baby
slimy with eyes that see too far inward
you remain safe inside the skin of your house and marriage
I turn back the sheets in many hotel rooms
captured by the flat afternoon light
your tongue lashes the inside of my mouth
into the messy bleeding beginning of us
ending

Isolation Rooms

here there was no way of telling time
so time was all that you had, the lights flickered dull orange
burnt pumpkins on the ceiling.
you woke up thinking of a hand on a distant thigh,
how the hours had felt round and safe as apples
and when you told him he was beautiful
he took both your hands and gave them back to you.
his eyes were blue and sad as blown glass.

when he came you promised not to die,
you examined the skins of your knees, pink
through the holes of the blanket, crouched together
like two bald heads, vulnerable.
the pages of dreams on the cement floor
were those of a child's, and you were embarrassed by it all,
from the first pill to the sound of ambulances.

that afternoon he had held you
until he became thin
and the parapraxis of his pocket watch fallen to the floor
of your apartment could have meant, after all, nothing.
he held you and in your mind turned brown and grey
like a chimney, and the smoke wrapped him up
and took him away.
later you sat in blue pyjamas, slept,
threw up charcoal in a thin soup in the sink.

perhaps you wanted to stay, in the morning
when the psychiatrists arrived with quick strides,
their bodies were tight, their laughter was louder

than another woman's tears, than the shuffle of a medicated man.
you were perfectly silent, in the green room
you felt like a found child.
if the bed had been wider or more comfortable,
you might have said something to stay, but when he came,
folding his leather jacket by the door
its collar cream and furry as a sleeping rodent,
you made the promise
and his hands made circles on your back.

for days afterwards you slept and woke but the walls
weren't green or cement, and the dreams you had
were those of a lost adult.
and when you came home you seemed further away than ever
and his silver pocket watch lay like a polished pebble on your floor,
ticking like a heart, and your thoughts began to darken again
like charcoal.

Thinking of Leaving

thinking of leaving
I arrive at another hotel lounge
circle the piano player with the starved shoulder blades
plot my approach of the men in shadows where they sit
sunk at the bowls of their tables
potted plants crawl over their faces, their call
is quieter than silence
their eyes level off above their drinks
I stand uncertainly
the men don't smile, they hide their teeth
bare them in their eyes

perhaps I will leave you for these marble floors
with their thickening white veins
a ladies bathroom where I am mirrored
ten times over from every angle
there is no reason to be nervous, there is after all
no chance of winning
the men carry briefcases as shields
I laugh at them and take a sample of their money
liquefy in their arms
feel them press up between my thighs like bookmarks
marking the place
the place to return to

you would look askance at this, you would look
from a certain angle wounded and soft
eyes lashed thickly as a child's
I think of you circling corners along that strip
with its girls decorated pink and blond

their tight closed lips
I can see the teeth in their eyes
feel the delight tickle upwards from between your thighs
noisier than sound

thinking of leaving, I consider
silver Mercedes' and blue-eyed dentists and suicide
in the meantime you arrive, you twist the doorknob
I step automatically towards you
you stuff my mouth full and silent with money
I like the taste, I let you stay
you destroy each coming day
I squeeze out sometimes between your hands and search
the rest of the world in hotels and restaurants
men like shadows with no mouths and rain-tired eyes
they pass like driven ghosts between my hands
they think of leaving

When It's Over

perhaps one day you'll find something
on an analyst's couch or in a textbook or
in the bluish beckoning smile of some girl
waiting for someone like you on a corner
of that long straight street
where streetlamps throw down pale carpets on the sidewalk
and there are many alleys to choose from
sidestreets gloomy with the overhangings of trees
someplace where there will be
no steady creeping sound of cars
footsteps pounding porch stairs, the jangle of keys
a woman's voice
to raise your head, cause your eyes
to sink to the color of sludge
no alarm to reduce to thin Kleenexes your quivering hands
your staining fingers

your tongue and my mechanical mouth race against the day when
obsession will tire of its furious treadmill
love will realize it never understood
the meaning of its own name

sad that when it's all over
you can look so old
your middle-aged face preposterous on my pink pillow
your hand fallen away and shirttail
wedged back into the trousers that never quite came off
the hallucinatory softness of your mouth
firms now into a line
and all the staggering jigsaw pieces
shift and slither beneath my unskilled hands

I Never Promised You

in that other country
you would wear a wool coat
the color of evening skies, your arm would be heavy as a branch
under snow, perhaps we would have heard ourselves laugh
and been surprised.
on sharp mornings we would step out on balconies,
inhale razor blades, embrace
under the dwarf of a sun, turning
in a sky the color of goosefeathers. we would wear thick coats,
walk for miles, lovers suddenly, not cripples.

how many white balloons have you filled
twisting the rubber tubes with your teeth
promising roses
the graves of dead poets
a divorce? a divorce so imminent had I shaken you
it would have dropped out of your mouth like a pebble,
it would have rolled off the tip of your tongue
where it lodged.

we would buy flowers and lay them on Tolstoy's grave,
each bloom a heart, lay out the stems
like the notes of a keyboard, and the country would light with flowers,
would blaze with flowers. and there,
hidden behind your back, behind that grove of trees,
the promised rose garden.

Into the Blue Room

the blankets are cold and woollen and a newspaper from another city
lies folded on the bedside table
you ease open a map of England, it carpets half the floor
my finger traces where you walked with your heart between your legs
you grasp my hand, your heart stiffens
and travels back to the solace of walks on green moors
the sound of thunder after a morning sky
the whip of an umbrella and the slick grapeskin of your raincoat
you are filled with more bridges and countries and dead girlfriends
than I have been given days to grieve or to laugh running
with my heart in my hand out of the blue room
away from the critical memento of a country you hated
schools that choked you silly with wide-striped ties and uniforms
you want to run with your heart bursting in the sheath
of another's hand, another's mouth
into which you leap and disappear

Projections

and it may be that you learned nothing, it is possible
to be exhausted from this sleep, to remember nothing
except the oldness of his body reflected
in a restaurant mirror, retreating from you,
shoulders bladed in the blue sweater
hands dropped down in defeat or depression.
how narrow his face looked, blackened with strain,
the eyes false and mirroring, green stone,
green as water, shifting.

that last night he feasted
on the unveiling of a year of lies,
the membrane of delusion lifted away in his fingers
like a graft of skin, like a skein of silk,
like wings.
the lies you promised to tell with your hands folded
safely in his, while the walls of his office
blushed slowly pink over the months as if shamed.
hour after hour the fog of pills shut him out
til his face was a father's face, healer,
destroyer, lost in its grip of private darkness.

he said he had never met anyone
so tragically like himself.
in thirty years, who could say?
meanwhile he handed you secrets like presents after a journey,
the broken men, the wounded healers that so delighted
and frightened him, the simian men who lectured
at the front of conference rooms with calloused eyes.
theirs were names that rhymed and rolled

off the tongue, you harvested the sick convulsive sweetness
of his secrets about the doctors with their women patients
their curious fingers.

but before long it seemed that something ended,
the light rusted, you rose dazed from a year as if
from a long sleep and dreams of love,
dreams twisting into nightmares.
and there was the silver afternoon, the metal plate of the day
tearing aside the blanket of your Oedipal dreams,
tearing him away til the day was dull and the room empty
and the sky unmoved. and you sat in the middle of your bed,
not a child, with Daddy grey and bent in the bathroom mirror
looking terribly confused, his fingers tapping ten anxious thoughts,
old as myth.

Last Year

he called it the year of the long hallucination
this storm in the brain, this storm in the sky
this storm of words in the blue room
where patients sat in different positions on the couch.
it was the year undefined
until his analyst failed to fall in love with you
he saw the unworthiness of what he loved.

you would call it the year of lies.
mirrors smoked on every wall down the hallway
when he returned to his office
his face the color of bone
and a storm rose on the horizon of his consulting room.
you saw afterwards he had drawn coffins and steeples
on the inner leaves of your file, around your words,
that his pen was angry.

if it was your hallucination, on the final day
the storm of words would falter and silence at the door
as patient after patient walked away

Tuesday Afternoon

an earthquake at 3:05, for a moment there is light
trembling on the spines of medical books
the mysterious diaries on the top shelf, I redirect my eyes
when you unfold your legs and
there is a flush of warmth in the room.
your hand draws circles on a pad of paper
traces lovingly the diagram of an African village
to you these words we use are only words
to me they are still magic, each book a ruby key,
their bindings have not aged in years.

this year sees you at fifty
it sees you comfortable inside your cotton shirt
picking out jellybeans from a jar on the desk,
white or red or black
colors you explain to me, the innocence and passion
and the thing that frightens us most.
I can taste them inside your mouth, wet,
luscious with meaning.
the shape I form of you between my hands
is weightless, it stands between us
voluptuous like a vowel, a figure fluid
as you settle here, removed for this hour
from the dimensions of your life.
your smallest smile is still sharp with wonder,
and fifty seems a good age for you.

your office stays white like princesses,
as in fairy tales.
some days you laugh, some days your eyes harbor

a suspicion of wet, your legs are
crossed or uncrossed, your hands
are filled with pens or toy hearts or marble sticks.
sometimes you speak as if there were a child in the room
when there is only me.
I spoke for years as if there were a crowd in the room
when there was only you.
you survived the hatreds and the lusts,
black, red, you knew the colors.

when light shattered across the floor
and briefly there was thunder between us, if your eyes
had held water it would not have spilled
and when we peeled aside the dreams the skin underneath
was still young. when all was black
you smoothed aside the words and said, It's there,
the light, when you want it
it'll be waiting for you—
and a certain peace came into your eyes,
that this was no different, that this was so different
yet every bit the same, and your hands stilled with satisfaction.
you did this without touch
so that all around me your hands stood
shaped like shelters, all around me there was room
and after each hour the hallways outside were like caverns
and around the corner and down the stairs
there lurked as always, light,
as ever, light.

Green

and already the leaves have arrived,
my doctor, that blur of green you spoke of four years ago
thickened while you sat, spread in your chair in the sun,
children scuffing bicycles down the alley to the grocery store.
it was not really green, you said, but rather
a haze of green, a fog of green,
a thought of green you could only call light.

I awoke from a dream panicked
thinking I'd missed the arrival of the leaves.
a landlady was taking me from room to room,
each one barren and small and filled
with the sound of typewriters. there was a view
of a beach in the distance, the encroachment of a wave
like a finger, spray hitting the empty shore,
a foreign beach the color of dust.
the trees were black arms holding up the sky,
crookedly. along the sidewalk in front of the building
that fine mist, that vague rain of green had gone,
and the branches were bent with a new burden of leaves.

four years ago we had word-associated this thought of yours,
this green that wasn't there,
back when mysteries were still abundant
and could be uncovered. yesterday everything was plain
and unbudging as a jug sitting in the sun.
the beach was the color of your shirt, sand,
the color of your face new to the sun.

in the morning there was no way of telling

if the leaves had come, since there were only buildings,
every room a bleak room. the phone rang loudly
while you, my doctor, went hunting in the park for the hint
of green, the cloud of green you'd held in your mind
for four years, the green that was still mysterious
and therefore solvable, the green that failed to exist.
it breathed along the backs of your thick white hands
as the phone rang in my chest
without a sound, and you groped further and further
down the beach with the voice of the sands.

Hearts

it is evening now, six floors below
the fountains sound, across the treetops
people move with movements they own in these apartments,
the weight of life along their spines.
and we have come to our termination.
five years would appear a long enough time,
yet the length of an hour is such a short distance,
such a long way to have travelled beside you.

at the beginning you said
I could be angry with you, you would not break
under the force of anger, crack like a dish on a wall
of floating faces. after a while
I no longer imagined you going away after the sessions,
sobbing like a child
until you mended.
later you said, I am not your father,
but everyone, limitless. I must remain
limitless. how young you were
when we first started, forty-five,
it seems impossible you were that young then. in your office
the same ivy as five years ago falls to the floor,
and nestled among the plants by the window like an Oriental gardener
a clock marks the minutes, the steady pulse of your eyes.

through twenty seasons
you changed imperceptibly, lost a certain fleshiness
around your mouth, your face grew smaller,
more a face than a vision, human,
a restful slant to your shoulders.

no life could be long enough to contain the desired hours,
the light across your cheeks, this wrestle
with an unruly self and its corridors of unconsciousness.
week to week your hands moved like the hands
of the clock on the windowsill,
the nib of a pen chattered between your fingers,
the air grew musty with confessions.
summer stood beyond the blinds, a fragment
of five other summers,
before autumn your favorite time of year,
the slow tender heartbreak of one season
leaking into another, the thin rainbow of cold
shivering in the air.
this that made you sad.
and your sadness that filled my heart.

for a moment today you held your face in your hands
above the crayons and the peacock display
of felt pens on the table, held it up like a child surprised by
the weight of its own physicality,
unconsciously consoling.
off in the distance, two parents stood,
light draining from their faces, arms no longer lifted.
the miles masked their faces, a grief of warm blood
thinned to mist, their hands resigned. this did not stop
me wanting to fulfill you, in some way
all those white thick pleasures of the men were meant
to be your pleasures, to comfort some slender sadness
in you which showed when light twisted through the blinds,
some loss that aged your cheekbones and gathered close
the space between your eyes.

this afternoon
you were in the mirror, climbing the stairs behind me, I saw

I have never been able to recognize you,
love being no less difficult here than elsewhere
with the two figures on the horizon, perhaps more so
with every person you assumed for me,
every face you wore
except your own face. it's the small things I see:
the soft webs of hair over your forehead,
the sensual fond twist of your smile,
your eyes the color of fields under heavy rain.
still I do not know how you lived
these past five years of your life, which mornings
were sensitive and weakest to confrontation,
who or what you lost,
your private human moments.

so what they say is true,
I carry you away inside me,
though it frightens me to be centreless
through the days and weeks that inhabit this world.
my impeccability
is something I fear I will fail at
but my own failure at least,
and counting the claimed parts of myself here,
tonight, the absences seem no more numerous than
the absences of others walking about in the world,
and the present pieces more valuable
for their difficulty. this then
is your silver self inside me and I hope for you
some impossible lack of disturbance,
some constant love, the persistence of attachment,
at least that you do not offend
against yourself.
one day we might yet touch

the figures on the horizon, find their thin aged skins
transparent in our hands.

in Cantonese
there are two words for happiness:
hoy sum:
"open heart". in Cantonese
I listened to my aunts in their struggles
out of radiant schizophrenia, out of the silver flying dreams
of thermoses hurled against walls when I was a child,
sex in mirrors, devils behind the shower curtains.
yet I heard them talk of happiness.
perhaps it was enough
that their hearts opened for a single moment
to let in a glimmer in this dance of darkness,
in the perceived mockery of faces on the street,
perhaps it was enough
to know once the contents of a heart, opened.

today you said, chin cradled in your hands,
that you didn't think I would die now if I didn't come back,
and your mouth was the shape of a question, a speculation,
the delicate eggshell of a hope. my doctor,
if I could I would leave you
with an armful of tiny silver metallic hearts
for you to pluck and shape through all your afternoons,
and every one of them
would be open.

Father

you fall through a shower of splinters and light
you dance with glass embedded arms
ten feet tall in my dreams, disguised perhaps
but look at how small I have become
in this bathroom stall
beside a man with blood on his elbow
the striped belt of his bathrobe braces my arm
the needle bounces in my flesh
for the first time you leave my thoughts
you who crowd my dreams wearing different bodies
you who walk through doors of glass
and survive
you who fall through skylights
I walk naked through many rooms
you stand cold as a vision
you leave me
I push you through glass doors in my dreams
through skylights
my father with the dark face, you appear more handsome
in dreams than in life, I hold up to you the handle
of a child's mirror

547 East 21st

light turned in the spokes of your tricycle
to the store where children with heads shining like new dimes
gathered, their faces dizzying over candies
shaped like marbles, firecrackers.
this was the home of the boy with the blond curls
who was complicitous to your lies
when you lost that red barrette in the schoolyard,
sunk somewhere in the sand, and was afraid,
and the children gathered around with pieces of sky
showing through faces aged with sympathy.
you followed the fancy of the light
and found yourself home each time, at a house cased in stucco
the color of broken beer bottles.
today they have torn half the fence away,
and a door sits like a sullen silence
in the basement where there was no door, only warm
unrenovated darkness. but through the fence crookedly
the weeping willows, the tree drowsy with honeyplums
that cushioned those years, their skins golden and furred inside,
cracking under the cold water
from the tap, bursting thickly through buttery seams,
the flesh slippery within.
the hardwood worn down
beneath your feet, the slant of the ceiling
and the sun that stung your eyes
back to dark sleep. your youngest aunt in the living room,
feet crossed over the armrest
like lotuses, and two other aunts crowded into the back room
where they watched the mountains, low blue crests to the north.

the afternoons clung together marked with the urgency
of berries and malnourished apples
that dropped green to the grass. and evenings
the sounds of the neighborhood couple engaged
in their usual after-dinner fight, the pins in the woman's hair
flashing the late light when it wandered over the back yards,
and always after her smile at the window, like a bit of the sunset
caught in her teeth.

Moving Day

all that year the shapes of women moved
in their yellowed rooms in the old folks home
across the alley. you swore
you heard them creak, like branches that blew
thinking they were leaves, when the winds
beat the windows with the bell of an alarm clock,
and you dreamt of highrises slumping down,
lengthening on the sidewalk, and all the glass blown away, and
every bedroom open to you.
in the building across the street
the windows of the penthouse shook and shimmered
like jello at a finger's touch. as a child
you wanted to leave no prints
but to preserve its slick surface like the surface
of something valuable, a photograph,
a silk kimono. summer exploded green
from every willing tree, surrounding you with life.
you wrote and threw away
your life along with the three-legged table
from your father's study.
because the trees changed over the seasons you said
you had changed, though your clothes were still ordered
into two closets to denote two lives, the day life
and the night life, like H. who divided her meals equally
into two plates, eating one then the other,
so neither personality would starve.
this was a small room like her basement
where she cooked tofu dinners and talked
about the sizes of penises she'd been with,
blue mascara stuck like a feeler to her cheek,

and read her manuscript aloud from a shoebox,
and tried to give you sweaters when you left
so you would not be cold.
a room this small already populated with this many
bad dreams caused other tenants to complain about the noise.
they were sure they heard screams
spacing the tapdance of typewriter keys.

Freud, At 20 Maresfield Gardens

a bicycle propped against the fence,
a dog in the garden echoing the yapping of Lun
as she skipped from your arms to the crackling grass.
you had a pummelled face,
little arms poking like sticks
from a sea of blankets and pillows,
behind glasses your eyes glinted, as if
holding back the pain of a chuckle.
when a camera caught you unprepared by the pond,
you were pointing at fish, perhaps a water spider,
leaning dangerously forward, you looked
peaceful as any old man, liberated of followers
and itchy blankets and a too-soft couch.
you might have been dressed in shorts,
a fishing rod propped nearby, your companion agreeable
and sunlight in the sky.

we moved through your house
in whispers. a woman wearing a wool coat sniffed
and snorted through each room, from emotion or cold.
then your study, the spread over the couch
patterned like jewels, a scarlet cushion in the centre
like an eye set in a forehead,
Egyptian figures prodding animals
or posing with sloped fleshy shoulders,
cloths slung on hips, spines pulled erect
by baskets on their heads.
a mask beside your arm lay ragged
where it ended mid-throat, gathered and mounted on a soft cloth,
faintly smiling.

We Thought Ourselves Unmoveable

but these were days that lost you in antique stores
on the other side of the narrow Thames,
waves tired in a slow-turning sun.
you bought spoons with reedy handles
in a lined case, learned to identify
white hornbeams by the feathers on their leaves,
hairs as silken as those on a forearm,
a peppermint cloud of laden branches
thrown side to side by the wind.
we walked for miles past quince trees and rooms
with crescent-shaped curtains, alleys golden and grey
as tiger's-eye in the rain, slick as stone.

evenings, cigarette in hand,
you waited on the back step
for a hedgehog, a flight of rooks
to ink the sky. neither came, only sleep
pulling at the corners of your eyes,
could draw you inside to the warmth of the kitchen
with the reluctance of tugged taffy.
and when we left for the bus, hung in balance
between our twin suitcases, your eyebrows
went diagonal with sadness. the man threw your cases
in and you turned to follow their flight.

Eyelids

the car stopped there, we scattered
into the farm, halos of sun spotting our eyes,
to see the ostriches. they came from the bottom of the hill
and their second eyelids came around also,
white as milk, shells of bone china,
flickering against vision. you spoke to them
in words as warming as wood
while the frightened dog yapped in the hay,
tail vibrating, black and white and tattered,
ears worn, face a ragged blade.
you stood still, talking some language
of comfort. the last rays of sun
ignited the ends of your hair,
isolated tufts the same texture
as the hairs on the throats of the ostriches,
untouchable, flashing peacock blue as they turned
down the hill to the edge of the farm.
one staggered back up to nod at you, the disk of its second eyelid
running back and forth like a plate set on its edge,
but when it bit you you said nothing. the sun began to set
slowly from the top of your forehead to the bottom
of your farmer's clothes; the ostriches huddled together,
heavy on the reeds of their legs,
eyes closed over like clouds.
you came back from the kitchen glowing and holding your fingers
this far apart, replicating the thickness of an ostrich eggshell,
anxious that I should not miss this,
or anything. it was your hurt hand
on the steering wheel that drove us home.

The Smaller Life

it was a schoolgirl you wanted, with a still white face,
crossing the bridge between Eton and Windsor,
a peppermint girl swinging a bookbag,
the grey Thames under her feet,
the swell of stone under her feet. a striped schoolgirl
with tears the taste of grapes
and a body full of imaginings

but Peter in the chapel
with his curious clammy hands, those flint eyes
selected you from across the courtyard,
across three quarters of a million pounds of stone and pebble,
by the Founder's Statue where you stood
on gold pieces. Peter with the moist eyes
took you behind the organ, up
triangles of stairs, where the boys' crosses hung.
outside, split sides of flint
shone like eyes in the courtyard, and on the Windsor bank
bluebells under every tree,
and statues with the stomachs of angels.

it's a smaller life now,
too narrow a life for the flourishing of words,
for the vines and accidental blooms of language
to overtake silence. while your wife
sleeps her voluptuous sleep, you sense how life has shrunk,
and your mouth droops like an unchecked eyelid,
a moment's unrecoverable banishment of self.

"Who Died of An Apparent Suicide Late Last Month"

now we wonder
if there were edges involved,
if it shone like rock silver blue
under rain, if it bit you with the flavors
of cinnamon and lemon, the burgundy of blood
along the sides of your tongue. and when it came
if it came gently. it is the afternoons
we remember, the indulgence of your tie flaring flowers
across your shirt, both arms flagging the back of the couch,
the grains of strength in your face and those eyes
breaking against laughter. late Fridays
in wilted downtown heat, leggy young secretaries bent over desks,
the strain of a radio,
you in your glass office. when you went east
we were jealous as children, your life was a rack we saw
hung heavy with silver spoons, every thorn filed blunt
with money. behind your back
we called you King.

we wonder how long it took
for everyone to dress for the funeral, what shade of black
was black enough, who designed
your wife's dress. it was the strength in you
we trusted, the slightly squashed nose, the full throttle blue
of the eyes, and the softness we laughed over—
the vanity that threatened the shaped mouth,
that hint of stupidity in the lines of the jaw,
your inheritance. now we do not know
how it came when it came, if it smelled spicy like blood,
if it was the slow vanilla muffle of drugs,
if the bathroom bloomed yellow and red

from the slick of metal in your hand,
what the pain said
when it spoke. if it was like going blind
in all your senses. we cannot see from here
your last thought that stood for an instant like a gull
against the watery sky, when you walked forward with the life
loosening from you.

Coming Home

coming home, you counted one person dead
for every year you were away in Singapore
eating rice and vegetables, standing by the side of the road
where the thinness of the people swelled to fill the streets
under a hood of heat.
you returned with a camera and a pair of socks slowly stained
the color of your shoes, expecting nothing,
not the rain that lay like glass outside the motel window,
or the cold through your cotton shirt. seeing nothing
but one friend hanging by a leash from the bridge,
puffy as a purple fig.
listen, you said in the parking lot outside,
the silence, listen to it, and I saw it cut you
with its high horrible delicacy, its vicious thinness,
so much silence to shatter you could hardly stand it.
so this my country, you said, and your eyes pulled tight
and your laughter forced sound after sound in the air.

Not Staying

all along you said you would leave
if you could find another country, some place
with no postcards and many newspapers,
They'd publish nothing about the rest of the world
but its crimes, you said,
they'd want me to think I was happy being away,
that I was better off,
and you laughed, the sound clotting your throat
like cream, the kind of laugh that afterwards
people remember where they were when they heard it,
what they were doing,
if they had laughed with you to keep you company.

in one photograph you are smiling hard
into the face of the camera, as if to make sure
we could see your teeth and be able to identify you,
later, when they found you and cut you down.
wherever you were that day it was sunny,
the picture was overexposed
so you stood against an anonymous background,
your face split open by your smile,
the arm of a sweater hanging over your shoulder
like the arm of a friend not inside the frame.

Telephone

it was morning here when you called, wild turkey
bottles behind the flounce of your bedskirt,
the sun a glare in the face of the sky.
what a time for it to be sunny,
you said, when it's been dark
for days. the bitterness edging out
the jersey accent, your voice long distance
flavored with lemons and oranges. your citrus voice.
here the apartment was slept in and stifled, I pulled in
a sheet of the blue sky to cover my knees
and a measure of scotch in a glass so we could talk
a similar language. eight years without a drink
and now these turkeys shaking their wattles
on soggy labels under your bed, and your voice tilting
and after an hour stumbling like a kid ballerina
in her first toe shoes. you said you would
kill yourself on american thanksgiving day:
a plastic bag over the head,
the thirty six bottles of hard liquor in the attic,
the gun store a pleasant afternoon stroll away.
and so many windows, like blank invitations.
during that morning hour while the sun slanted
across the digital clock over the leather furniture
and into the bed my heart sank like fine sand
down the hourglass of my body til I was lead
and could not lift myself.
you said you'd call again in three days
and didn't. two weeks of silence.
on thanksgiving day in your country,
turkey feathers and necks littered the yard.

Waking in Toronto

nights of green marble lounges and nights
of white bathroom tiles and nights of absence,
hands that try to take you as if you're fifteen again.
your feet are bloody roses of heat
and pain, on the streets
you meet an error of lemon and grape pills.
and the neons of Yonge St. flash the color of your clothes
while snow falls all around
onto empty university grounds.

and you wake to your life
with feet that have walked the coals of dreams,
the 600 windows of the hotel empty.
at six AM a sun bursts through the shell of cloud
goldening your arms and kneecaps,
igniting the hairs on your calves. and on this bed
are all the unforgotten men.

Dressing Up

drops of perfume dangle from your fingers
like yellow pearls, you smear them
in snail's tracks along your arms
between your breasts
a stranger pats his hands on your back
a serpent climbs the poles of your lungs to uncoil into a sob
your brain is dizzy with pills that dissolve
into the watermelon underflesh of your tongue
every glass reflects the mask slipping
a thin strand of hair or a smudged mouth
you are beginning to see your seams
it is autumn and the trees strike live matches around your home

The Restaurant

Sante Fe walls and the ribbon lips of a waitress
with torn hair, a bartender with glistening nose
you are working with a script of blank pages tonight
opposite a pair of eyes which cue
your next smile or pale giggle
the businessman leaves in his Porsche, with a swing
of his trenchcoat and the night navy of his suit
he turns down the west side street back to his house
with its rich Chinese wife
and solar-heated doghouse
one day you too may marry into your desire
for now you approach his client
the blue eyes of diamond tiles beneath your feet
he lies on the bed with his flame-ruined body
here in this desert of emotion where the baked sand
of the walls warms you, he nods
and you slip your hand into his lap
swallow past the parchment of your throat
your fingers try to refrain from bruising
as you guide him towards mirage

Nineteen

the men file home with flowers in their hands
rubbery petals scent the rain, it is late
the hours pass in dreams, you wake
after the shade of night is tugged down
the men walk past in white trenchcoats, asking directions.
it is February and the flowers in the grocery stores
are dying in their white pails, the grocer is bending down
and picking them up, taking them inside,
taking them away.

the men say they love you, your hair
falls over their alcoholic faces in slick blue curls
you kiss them randomly. oh, the men:
precious as ivory,
dead flowers uprooted in their hands.
all you have to show for them is a few roses,
a smattering of pills in the green glass ashtray,
but he calls you Baby Girl and you watch porn movies together
on the white leather sectional, pop antibiotics and drink scotch
when there's nothing else around.
you know he's your last chance.

he keeps pictures of you in his drawer
your artificial hair whipping against the camera
your model's pout damp with hunger
your eyes like tombstones, black and white.
upstairs the beds are quiet.
at three AM you smash the twisted iron gate and run to the cab
to a driver who assaults you with hard hands
you say nothing, tell no one

is it not enough that you got away?
four AM and you sit in the hallway listening to the rain
emptying out through the drains in the balcony
a stench in the bathroom
knees drawn up in that classic position, you're alive
which should be enough for anybody, but already
you've begun to stop wanting
and more and more men in their ivory skins pass you
in the increasing night, carrying away flowers til all is dark.

Needles

alone on the sofa, five bent spoons
arched curiously on the tabletop
a squiggle of blood swims up the syringe
the liquid burns your arm
presses along your shoulders with the weight
of a dozen gold bricks
the man plugs in another porno
limbs of flesh enter and separate
your eyelids float down black discs
a cotton silence as the nose of the needle
sniffs and searches under skin
your veins are glass vessels calling
even his girlfriend looks up from her needle to say
you look so lost

February Dawns

light sliced up roses in the arid morning, light
crawled in through a torn sky
and landed on teacups sour with whiskey and lipstick
a hand shaking in midair.
between a wall of mirrors and the spray of dead roses
you stroked the lilies, they splayed on their stalks
like the folds of genitals, tough and smooth
while twin beds heaved with goosefeathers
and the bathroom door slammed, slammed.
he wouldn't let you take anything of value:
the coffee table with its tiny villagers wading through rice fields,
the hidden butterflies in the English paintings,
the piano with the stuck key.
still, when he called you fled to him as if chased
into the unheated marble elevator that mirrored your panic
and eagerness and your harsh lipstick. you ran
past the lights on the tree in the garden
through the iron gate, into the oval rooms
where you stood all night watching the cabs drive by
the rain dropping down like silver money
where you stood in the morning above the fleshy curves of the sea
watching the cabs turning at the shoreline
and feeling safe in their passing.
you could see the sun struggling through the fog,
weak as a heart.
often though the opening of another day found you
on your hands and knees in the bathroom, while he traced
the slapping patterns your palms made against the tiles,
and smiled, and sipped his cigarette.
his eyes flashed by like steel-blue Cadillacs

the clock in the hallway chimed on and on
you hoped he would wake with the light on the wrong side of the
house
car and wallet and keys gone and dressing gown
bunched at the waist, wake to the terrible profusion
of his life, the bedside phone
clumsier with cords and buttons than he had ever recalled it.
you got out of bed only to accommodate the vomiting
that came finally like a gift.
at five AM you tried to leave, your hands pushing away
his kisses like blows, pushing at the buttons to the elevator,
relying on the taxis being there and being compassionate.
the ocean had parted and for an instant you saw
a dozen yellow trunks turned up and one back wheel
desperately spinning on the horizon as the sun rose.

New Horizons, U.S.A.

he called from the airport, Winnipeg was cold
so he drove south, Marilyn Monroe flaring across his tie,
the trademark skirt, hands pressed damply to thighs,
the waxen smile.
I felt glamorous then,
drinking soda water and good scotch and talking about
my trip to London, a city he remembered only
for its bad plumbing. at New Horizons
under the cut glass lanterns, the moss warmth
of the pool, he paddled after me balancing a rubber raft
with a psychologist in a black T-shirt
who kissed the cuts on my wrists, the initials
carved in my thigh, her hurried hands
tying my wet hair to the nape of my neck,
strapping my ankles in stirrups
as the red ball of the sun rolled into the forest,
and the lights spun down.
I cried into her crotch, the ceiling turned a slow
merry go round as body after body floated over me.
afterwards, in the confusion of blow dryers and makeup
and used condoms in the bathroom,
he failed to recognize the shape of me
under the white light bulbs, what I looked like
while untouched.

Monkey on the Ceiling

you can hear the structure of the world, cracking
a mirror and a Monkey with limbs crooked
stapled to the ceiling
eyes dead as raisins
you are afloat on the ceiling, wreathed with the clutch
and clamour of bodies
the trees outside with leaves wet and turning
the heavy sound of his breath on the porch
an ominous jut to his hip, you spin
on the points of your heels in the grass
Monkey, caught on a mirrored ceiling
tackled by bodies with many white hands
that spread you wide, position a limb or an eyelid
you study this spreadeagled reflection
carefully place an elbow attractively
feel the rough skins of men and women beneath your fingers
you watch his mouth dip at a stranger's body
a shadow against the wide smooth windows
you watch his mouth bob anxiously
and the silence, you watch the silence
her hair tickles your thigh, the dumb giggles parade
from her mouth in high blond notes
Monkey dances on the ceiling, you dance
topless in a roomful of strangers
he pulls your clothes off and stuffs them in his pockets
you toss your body to the sound of the night
the animal rearing of the bodies around you
the music is the old money in his eyes, purchasing you
the music is in your fat nipples kicking up to his lips
his tongue erases you and all the trees have taken on eyes
Monkey strikes another pose in the centre of the matrix

of arms and legs and the tops of strangers' heads
you are slowly being kissed stroked battered dumb
you follow him with the belief he has something you want
you crouch in every corner, Monkey, you walk with drink
in hand through inherited houses, play his daughter's piano
let him tear your body a little wider harder
with his hands his groans
you are crucified to your own reflection, perfect
in his sated eyes drowsing with boredom

Room of Tears

you showed me pictures of mollusks
and sea urchins, some spiked, some flabby
as wombs, the sand a sifting floor.
you were the fifth person to enter the room of tears
in centuries, this cave named
for stalactites and stalagmites worn
to the shapes of teardrops.

we talked until you were ready for sleep,
brass bed and black pyjamas.
your body straight in sleep, sheets pulled to chin,
had the blurred curves of a mummy in the British museum,
wrapped in bandages the color of parchment.
yet your face was alive as a lamp,
pupils wide to take in the remaining light.

it took nights to learn your body,
the way your lips pushed together in pain
or joy, the sounds you made with your mouth gagged
when threats and whips slammed the wall above your head,
what color horror painted your eyes.
your fingers furled and opened like soft creatures
underwater, an Enya tape on the stereo
and behind my eyelids the English countryside flashing by
the way it did that spring
from the back of a sports car, endless green,
and lambs who dropped tails like feces on fields
bordering the stones at Avebury.

it was the silence
of the deep sea you loved, the cut of the coral,

the creatures that breathed with their bodies
as if their whole bodies were genitals, feeling, pulsing,
opening. tears fell
on your shoulders from the ceilings of caves,
and fish lit the water white
as happy brides.

Night After Night

the big hand of the clock tugs up
towards midnight and around and
down. Mariah Carey on the stereo and the cabbies drive,
thumping wheels and snapping fingers,
speeding through West End, Shaughnessy,
to the rears of houses with carports
and basement doorbells,
the tops of highrises with frail balconies,
lobbies with mirrors and without.

you buy me roses and amitriptyline and sometimes a shirt
to wear home. under the Coca Cola lampshade
we plough through the last case of wine.
it's your birthday and you are sleepy with medication,
swapping stories, telling lies. the lies
the only good things, railings to clutch
on your way down the staircase to sleep.

it's not loneliness
anymore, these greedy evenings of wine,
Halcion-induced nights and brain damaged mornings.
I think it is hard sex,
men crying when they're chained to bedposts,
when the sight of a nipple can bring climax over their hands,
bring shame like a shutter
slamming down.

your cuffs and harnesses make me sad in the bathroom,
sad while reading Punch magazine on the toilet seat,
sad while telling jokes like K. at cocktail parties

here and in Toronto, face tomato red from booze,
pleading for Tylenol for the fourth time.
when you fall asleep at your own party
from too many antidepressants, a jug of roses
spills over the table and balloons start to follow
their strings down and deflate.

I come
and don't like it.
that night you dream about Chinese pagodas with walls
around them that you can't penetrate.
I dream about cutting you up
and stuffing you into the garbage chute
after following the instructions on the door:
drain all garbage, wrap and tie tightly, no bottles
please because they might break
on their way down.

Indian Summer, 1991

we bought bags of clothespins, toured the love shops
that indian summer. you received invitations
to threesomes, gave air-conditioned rides across the border
to clubs where condoms lay next to cutlery at dinner
(dancing to "Gloria" your hot hands
grazing mine, we told everyone you were my professor
and I was working for better grades),
condoms blue yellow pink like squashed flowers.
we blew them up, threw darts at them,
I missed wildly. we danced
(the lights the music cubing your face
red and silver, you shuffling your feet so seriously)
for hours. under sunbeams that fell
through october and november into the beginning
of december, women painted their melting eyes,
pushed their breasts up to where they used to be
(or never were), wore tennis whites beneath faces
shiny with vodka at one in the afternoon.
in Mack's Leathers, the riding crop the salesman showed us was
pink, he flicked its tongue at me
like a tease inside a smile. it was already winter
when we started this adventure, thinking we could find
our way home in the dark.

Ladies

yours was a name meant for sunlight and muslin, Marie,
not your poor body frescoed with veins zigzagging
from hips to ankles as though you are a clay sculpture
cracking, the cakes of your knees
denting the mattress with your weight,
Marie, sliding a pool of brandy into the hollow
of his stomach, laughing, laughing,
the glass empty in your hand,
the rim of the glass singing under your finger.
Marie with the damp, complicated tangle between your legs,
a foamy sea animal drowning between your legs.
It tastes like yoghurt, you say,
it tastes like ice cream,
and when he comes to you
your eyes close on him like locks and the only words you say are,
Vanilla ice cream, and he thrusts, staring at you.

staring at you, Marie, like there's something in you,
your brown eyes huge with makeup the color of stones
and shells on your lids, the color of the dress
I brought back from London, not thinking you would walk in
wearing that color on your face, or the sly droop
of a golden horn around your neck, tarnishing
like the necklaces and chains looped under your skin,
this horn for good luck between your breasts,
this horn like a fingernail, Marie.
Look, you say, he came wearing white
and we both wore black
but we're ladies, we're innocent . . .

Marie, cleaningwoman, your only real estate now
is in the geography of our bodies.
when you raise your face with a spiderthread
suspended from the corner of your mouth,
the necessary buttons of your nipples pointing
like thumbs from your chest, I tell you there is solitude
between the points of a triangle, listen,
but you expertly coax the pearly shower
from the centre of his body, you throw back your hair
in this familiar triumph, Marie,
the pearls falling like all the riches of the sea
from your fingers.

Afternoon #1

the screaming weight of me sinks into you
in one concentrated point of pressure
flowering red
a needle slides through your shell-pink nipples, still as silk
I watch your face
hair flung back on the carpet
roots turned up to betray the grey, you appear caricatured
glasses removed and nudged to safety several feet away
eyes myopically squinted, when they look up they are violet
and pungent

you pull out pictures of a woman corseted in black leather
boots strangling her thighs
she turns back to summon the man
crawling naked behind her, back humped like a dog's
the studs on her leash smile in the light
the studs on his collar grimace
your magazines show men with tenderized flesh
slash marks burning the skin
their bodies the texture of unbaked clay
the women are every size and appearance but their eyes
are uniformly modelled
leather sharpens the sloppiest silhouettes

your neck presses deeper into the floor, I can no longer see it
beneath my heel, I can barely hear you breathe
in the middle of the afternoon I start to laugh
while your face fills with blood and oxygen and I think of
puncturing you
in the cramped light between the pulled drapes

I run my hands into your hair
you are making me happy and I am
afraid of killing you here in this afternoon
where the laughter is real
where the neighborhood children outside shout their games

The Madman

his eyes are marbles soaked in fire and vodka,
there is no color to madness,
only the feel of him between wool sheets, in a room
with the windows nailed shut.
at five AM in the adjacent bedroom
he hears the sound of breathing, though there is no one there
and he sharpens a butcher knife, smiling.
and all I can think of is you, like a sickness in my breast,
as my heels sound down the dead-end streets,
as my shoes set off lights and alarms
strung along the gates of Kerrisdale homes.

his living room is a rink of polished hardwood,
a fire blazes his cheeks,
the poker is inches from his left hand
as he cuts and slashes at the wife who divorced him.
and all I can think of is you, you fill my stomach
like a child, I drink and drink
and sleep with the madman, I dance with the madman
in a room screaming with cockatiels, yellow, orange,
wings slicing many-bladed knives through the air.
he has made me his sweet deceit
in a fur coat, his reluctant Venus, and at the point of gratification
there can be no analysis.

his eyes are coated with pus and tears
his hands are swift with twenty years
of military training, and when the gun goes off
the taxi pulls away from the house into the blue night,
the velvet night, and the sparks are slivers of gold.

I think of you, it is not true
that you passed unnoticed, but you chose to gratify
and you can't analyze what you gratify.
when the madman stabs his invisible wife in the firelight,
when the madman crouches and leaps in the firelight,
I think of you, and a gratification worth ashes.